DON'T CALL ME CRAZY, CALL ME CEO

DON'T CALL ME CRAZY, CALL ME CEO

A Guide for Women Running Businesses While Managing Their Mental Health

ANGELA M MITCHELL

TITLE: DON'T CALL ME CRAZY, CALL ME CEO

First Printed: 2025

Editor: Leslie Cottrell

ISBN eBook: 979-8-9997380-0-4

ISBN Paperback: 979-8-9997380-1-1

Printed in the United States of America

DEDICATION

To the women who wake up every day fighting battles no one sees.

The women building businesses, leading teams, and chasing dreams,

All while silently juggling the storms of bipolar disorder, anxiety, or depression.

This is for you sis.

For the fierce ones who show up even when they don't feel strong.

For the brilliant minds that refuse to be defined by a diagnosis.

For the hearts that carry both ambition and vulnerability in the same breath.

You are not invisible, dear sister.

You are not alone.

And you are not broken.

This guide is my love letter to you.

May it remind you that you can lead, love, and thrive, fully and unapologetically, exactly as you are.

Much respect,

Angela M. Mitchell

TABLE OF CONTENTS

INTRODUCTION

WHY I WROTE THIS BOOK

Let me be honest with you right from the jump, this isn't a story wrapped with a bow, tied neatly with perfection and productivity hacks. Nah. This is a guide written from the messy middle. From meetings and breakdowns. From days when I felt unstoppable... and the ones when I couldn't even get out of bed. That's what this is, the lows, the darkness.

My name is Angela M. Mitchell. I am a CEO. I am a digital marketing strategist. A coach. A speaker. An international bestselling author. And I also live with bipolar disorder, anxiety, and depression.

For years, I hid behind the mask of "having it all together" while silently fighting for my sanity and battling the shame and stigma of my diagnosis. I thought I had to choose, either be seen as strong and successful or be honest about my mental health. I chose silence... until I couldn't anymore.

This book is for the woman who's building an empire while fighting invisible battles.

It's for the CEO who cancels meetings because she's emotionally depleted... the mompreneur who shows up for everyone else but feels like she's falling apart inside... the high achiever who's tired of pretending she doesn't need help.

Listen Sista. You don't need another self-help book that tells you to "just meditate more" or "think positive." No! You need real tools, fierce truth, and soul-deep encouragement from someone who *gets it.*

This is that book.

Inside, I'll share what I've learned, not just about surviving my mental health challenges but about thriving through them. I'll show you how I've built a sustainable business around my energy, not against it. How I've cultivated self-love, healthy boundaries, and powerful routines. And how I continue to show up, unapologetically, in both my healing and my hustle.

I promise, you don't have to be perfect to be powerful.

You can lead and still need help. You can rest and still rise. You can honor your mental health and still be a damn good CEO.

So, let's take this walk together.

Unmasked. Unashamed. And completely unstoppable.

With love,

Angela

PART 1

THE INNER WORK... LIVING & LOVING YOURSELF THROUGH IT

CHAPTER 1

The Day Everything Cracked Open

I wish I could tell you my story started with a lightbulb moment, some deep motivational quote, or a mountaintop meditation. But it didn't. It started on the floor. In the dark. With a panic attack that felt like it would never end. It started with me laying there begging for God to just take me away so that I would finally be free of the anguish I found myself in. I laid there on that floor all night crying and praying, ready for a sign, a breakthrough, a lifeline! Little did I know that everything would change for me in less than twenty-four hours.

It was January 4, 2020. I had been in a deep, numbing depression for nearly four years. My business was suffering. My relationships were strained. I was barely recognizable to myself. And I was tired of pretending I was fine.

That morning, I scrolled across a Facebook Live. A woman who I had been following for a few years was talking about healing and divine purpose. She said something I'll never forget:

"You already have everything you need to overcome what's trying to break you. You are selected, significant, and supplied by God." That was it for me, the crack that let the light in.

I have always known that God sends you who and what you need when you are ready, and not a second before. I had been praying and asking for so many years just for the opportunity to be seen and heard and had been wanting to tap into the online space for years. I was finally ready to move from the sidelines. Growing my faith and trusting that God was waiting for me to see myself was the motivation that got me to the other side of the darkness I had existed in for so long. And yes, I merely existed because there is no life where there is no hope.

Finally, I recognized and accepted that I had been struggling with my mental health for many years, so I got the help I needed to stop repeating the same cycle. I was diagnosed with bipolar depression, and generalized anxiety disorder, but the best part was that I finally had a name for the thing that had plagued me my whole life.

I was so thankful to finally understand the extreme depressive lows and crazy manic highs I had been going through. You see, what I didn't get at the time is that those breakdowns and low times were sacred invitations, the cracks where the light flooded the darkness, I thought I would die in.

Awakening

There's a moment, it could be a quiet one, or maybe a loud explosive one, when everything you thought you had under control finally falls apart. But this time, instead of pretending everything is fine, instead of stuffing it down or pushing through, you decide to stop.

You stop hiding it.

You stop fighting it.

Because, for the first time, you face it. All of it.

That moment doesn't feel good or look beautiful while you're deep in it. It feels terrifying. It feels messy. It feels like failure. But when you look back you realize, damn, that's the moment that everything shifted:

The very moment you give yourself permission to break, to let it go... and then rebuild again, piece by piece, this time *on your own terms.*

What Helped Me Wake Up

When I hit my rock bottom, these things didn't "fix" me, but they gave me a foundation, solid ground to stand on. They gave me clarity in the middle of my chaos:

- **Getting the Diagnosis**

  Finally having the words bipolar disorder, anxiety, and depression was a starting point that allowed me to say, *"Oh, okay. That's what this is."* That's when I stopped blaming myself for things I couldn't control. It gave my struggle a name. And from there, I could learn how to live with it instead of feeling lost inside it.

- **Releasing the Shame**

  I swear for the longest time I thought my mental health challenges were a flaw in my character. Like I just wasn't strong enough, disciplined enough, spiritual enough, woman enough. But I realized: "Girl, this is only one part of your story, not the whole thing. There is not one thing to be ashamed of." When I released the shame and ignored the stigma of having mental health disorders, I felt like a weight had been lifted off my shoulders, I was done carrying that weight.

- **Asking for Help**

  From therapy to prayer, from medication to journaling, I built a real support system. Not just one thing, *many* things, and most importantly, many people. They held me up while I pieced myself back together.

It's okay to ask for help, in fact, the biggest sign of your strength is knowing when you need support and going to get it.

Tips for the Woman Who's at Her Breaking Point

When you feel like you're crumbling, here's what I want you to know:

You are not too far gone.

You are not broken beyond repair.

You are just at your moment of awakening.

Here are three ways to walk yourself through it:

Say It Straight

Don't minimize it. Don't sugarcoat it. Don't whisper. Don't water it down or dress it up for other people's comfort. Stand on business and say it with your chest!

Whether it's rage, fear, sadness, or numbness, say it exactly as it is.

You can't move what you won't face.

Sit with yourself, write it down, say it out loud:

"I'm pissed off."

"I'm exhausted and overwhelmed."

"I don't feel like myself."

"I don't know how to keep going."

This isn't about collapsing and giving into it. It's about *facing it* head on so you can shift it. You can't heal what you won't acknowledge.

Ask for Help Before You Think You "Deserve" It

A few of the biggest lies we tell ourselves is:

"I'll get help when it gets worse."

"I don't want to burden anyone."

"Other people have it harder than me, so I won't complain."

You don't have to hit rock bottom to get support.

It could be therapy, medication, calling your good girlfriend, or just saying out loud, *"I'm not okay,"* those words are powerful.

It doesn't matter what you choose, just do it! You are worthy of care *right now girl.*

Not later. Not after you "earn it." Especially in your lowest moments, you need and deserve that help. The bravest thing you can do is let someone meet you where you are.

Stop Performing. Start Processing.

That mask you wear, the one that has you always being the strong one, the fixer, the overachiever, the go-to person, it's heavy. And you can't keep going that way, it's not sustainable.

I want you to take it off. Right now.

Give yourself permission to not have the answers. To not know the next step.

You don't have to lead with the perfect, polished version of yourself to move forward. Healing doesn't come from performing and pretending. Healing comes from processing and doing the work. From sitting with what's real. From letting yourself feel what you've been trying so hard to hide.

Your true strength lives right there: not in holding it together all the time, but in letting yourself fall apart long enough to rebuild a stronger, truer, you.

Your Turn: Journal Prompts: Let the Truth Speak

1. What am I pretending not to feel right now?
2. What would I say if I could be completely honest with myself, and with someone I trust?
3. What does "breaking open" mean to me? And what might be waiting for me on the other side?

Affirmations: For the Woman Rising Through the Ruins

- I am allowed to fall apart and still rise again.
- My truth is not too heavy. It is sacred.
- I am not my diagnosis. I am a masterpiece in progress.
- There is power in my pause, and healing in my honesty.
- Even in the breaking, I am becoming.

Your Cracks Are Not Your Weakness

The day everything cracked open was the day I started telling the truth, to myself, and then to others. If you're in that space right now, raw, vulnerable, unsure, feeling broken, know this:

You are not broken.

You are breaking free.

This is your beginning.

NOTES

CHAPTER 2

Embracing the Diagnosis Without Letting It Define You

I used to think that having a diagnosis somehow meant I was damaged goods. Bipolar disorder. Generalized anxiety disorder. Recurrent major depression. Those words felt like a punch in the gut, and I felt the color drain from my face when the doctor said them. His suggestions of counseling and medication nearly took me out.

It felt like I had been branded with the stamp *mentally unstable* across my forehead by some invisible committee. Hell no, I wasn't telling anyone about my diagnosis, not even the man I was in a relationship with; no one. I wasn't ready to deal with it, so I shut it out of my mind and kept going like nothing happened.

I smiled through meetings with my clients and their families, coached clients, and carried on with my life while quietly navigating extreme mood swings, sleepless nights, and paralyzing fear that I'd eventually "slip up" and lose everything.

But here's what I've learned along the way: **a diagnosis is information, not identity.**

It's a guide, not a prison. And the moment I stopped fighting the label and started understanding it... that's when things began to shift.

Self-Acceptance Without Self-Limitation

You can accept the truth about your mental health *without* feeling defeated. Why? Because this is about loving and accepting ALL of you. Every part, no matter what that looks like.

Your diagnosis doesn't erase your brilliance, your creativity, your leadership, or your destiny. No ma'am! In fact, it's part of what makes you the woman you are meant to be.

What Helped Me:

I Named It, So I Could Face It

When I finally received an accurate diagnosis, things started to become clearer for me. It was almost like a good wind came along and blew away the fogginess in my mind. Now, don't get me wrong, it didn't happen overnight, but I had the answers I needed to get started.

It gave me a framework to understand why I'd had such emotional highs and lows, such deep sadness followed by bursts of energy, such unpredictability in my emotional landscape. I stopped thinking I was crazy and started realizing I was *human*.

I Rewrote the Narrative

It was time to stop hiding and being embarrassed about something I had absolutely no control over. I also let go of the victim mentality I was holding on to so tightly. So, instead of saying "I am bipolar," I started saying "I live with bipolar disorder."

Words matter. I am not my diagnosis. I am a CEO, an author, a woman of purpose, who happens to navigate life with mental health challenges.

I Learned My Triggers and Cycles

Understanding how my moods move, what triggers my anxiety, and when I need extra support was crucial for my healing and helped me manage my life and business without either of them falling apart. Now I build *with* my brain, not against it.

When I am experiencing mania and my energy is through the roof, I use that energy to create something. Whether it's a digital product, workshop, or mini coaching groups, I make the best of that time and turn that energy into profit!

Your Turn: Reflection Prompts

1. What stories have you told yourself about your diagnosis or mental health?

2. How has shame shaped how you show up in your relationships or business?

3. What would it look like to see your diagnosis as a roadmap, not a roadblock?

Your Diagnosis is a Doorway

You don't have to wear your diagnosis on a tee shirt for the world to see or use it as a wall to hide behind. No ma'am! It's a *part* of your journey through womanhood, not the whole story.

You get to write what comes next.

NOTES

CHAPTER 3

NAVIGATING THE MOOD MAP

Some mornings I wake up ready to conquer the world. I've got my day laid out, five new ideas, and my power playlist ready to go. I'm productive, positive, and I feel like I can take on whatever the world throws my way.

Other mornings? I'm paralyzed under the weight of the covers, wondering why my heart is racing and my brain feels like it's buffering.

Yes girl, this is the reality of living with bipolar disorder, anxiety, and depression, unpredictability. But here's the game-changer, I stopped reacting to it... and started **tracking** it.

Once I began understanding my mood patterns, energy fluctuations, and emotional triggers, I was no longer caught off guard. I could prepare. Plan. Respond. *Lead.*

Mental health may not come with a GPS, but you can absolutely create a map.

Self-Tracking & Self-Understanding

When you understand your inner landscape, you stop labeling yourself as "lazy" or "inconsistent" and start leading yourself with compassion and strategy.

A Few Tips to Help You Navigate Your Mood Map

Start a Daily Mood & Energy Journal

It doesn't need to be fancy, but it should be focused and intentional. Just take 10 minutes each morning to jot down your mood. Do you feel nervous or anxious with high energy? Or are you sluggish and feeling low? Include your sleep quality and quantity. How did you sleep and for how long?

Take a few minutes during the day to check in with yourself. Did your mood change, are there any triggers around? Do it on your lunch break, between meetings, downtime, or whatever, just be sure to check in. Write both your triggers and / or wins. At the end of your day when you have calmed down, check your mood. Patterns will begin to emerge, and those patterns will become your power.

Identify Your "Tells"

When I'm in a season of mania my mood shifts sometimes show up as shopping sprees or jumping headfirst into something new. Like the day I decided to enroll in school and finish the remaining credits to earn my degree. I ran out for a quick trip to Rite-Aid, heard a commercial on the radio for Bryant and Stratton College, called from the parking lot, and was enrolled before I went in to grab my laundry soap. By the time my mania calmed down, I was half-way through the semester asking what the hell I got myself into!

You know what your signs are. Maybe for you it's when you start pulling back from people, places, and things you love, or overspending, or feeling invincible. These are often signs of an oncoming shift. Pay attention and track those early indicators so you can pause, reset, or ask for help.

On the flip side, when I was experiencing a depressive period, I had to learn to spot those signs as well. My lows would find me overeating and retreating from the world because I was embarrassed about all the weight I was gaining. There would be times when I was so depressed that I didn't get out of bed, bathe, or do anything other than sleep for days at a time. I would miss meetings, calls from potential clients, and my business would suffer.

But, once I started tracking my moods and recognizing the patterns, I was able to turn those low periods around by taking control of my nutrition and fitness. I got a trainer, changed my diet, and started using workouts to help with my moods. I got on a workout schedule and made sure I stuck to it. I lost weight, but I gained a better understanding of my triggers and how to handle them.

Plan Your Business Around Your Brain

Once I recognized my patterns and telltale signs of my mood shifting, I would use that manic energy to do something purposeful. I would create a course or new lead magnet, or maybe I would just get cute and record a few videos and batch content on high-energy days. Whatever it was, I made sure I used that energy productively.

You can schedule client calls when you're most clear-headed. Create systems (or hire support) to hold things down when your mood dips. Flexibility is your friend, build it into your business model. When you're feeling low, use that time to stay active, but also listen to your body and rest, reset, and recharge.

Journal Prompts: Track Your Truth

1. What signs show up when I'm beginning to spiral (up or down)?
2. How can I build a schedule that honors my natural rhythms?
3. What's one small habit I can start today to track my emotional health?

Affirmations: For Emotional Awareness & Grounded Power

- I honor the rise and fall of my energy with love and curiosity.

- Knowing myself is the key to leading myself.
- I don't fear my shifts; I understand and support them.
- I build systems that serve my peace, not just my productivity.
- Every emotion is valid. Every pattern is information. I am learning me.

NOTES

CHAPTER 4

THE DAILY PRACTICE OF STAYING GROUNDED

I used to wake up already drowning before I even opened my eyes. Emails, deadlines, social media notifications, and a to-do list longer than my patience. I'd go from zero to chaos before I even brushed my damn teeth.

That life? It wasn't sustainable. Especially not with a mind like mine, one that's wired for both brilliance and burnout. I would find myself spending hours on "busy work," but not really accomplishing anything. I would sit in front of the computer and zone out because my eyes were burning and I was overwhelmed and exhausted. Every part of my business suffered, and I wasn't making any money! I knew something had to change, fast!

The shift happened when I made peace my *priority*. Not as a luxury, not something I had to make time for, but as a non-negotiable. Now, before the meetings, the marketing, the momentum, I anchor myself. I ground my thoughts. I honor my nervous system.

Because being a CEO with mental health disorders isn't just about pushing through, it's all about **practicing presence** and grace for yourself.

Grounding Rituals That Keep You Centered

Staying grounded doesn't mean you'll never get overwhelmed. Life is going to happen no matter what you do. You must be prepared. That means you have practices that pull you *back* when the world, your thoughts, and your emotions try to take you out.

Three Grounding Tips That Changed My Life (and Business)

Create a Morning Flow That's Just for You

Every day before I look at my phone, check an email, or see what's happening in these social media streets, I set the tone for my day. I start with being grateful and thanking God the moment I realize I woke up to see another day, and before I open my eyes, I say a silent prayer of thanks. Then I get up and grab my journal and coffee and write my thoughts, intentions, and prayers for the day.

Even if it's just fifteen minutes to write in your journal, pray, stretch, breathe, sip tea in silence. Take that time for yourself and your sanity. Don't let the world in before you check in with *you*. That sacred time is your soul's seatbelt. Get up a little earlier so you have time before you must deal with the day.

Use Anchors Throughout the Day

Set alarms to pause and breathe. Keep the affirmations on your desk, have them on your phone, etc. Step outside for three minutes of sunlight. Step away from the computer, put your phone down, and just breathe. These mini habits bring you back to your body when your brain starts racing.

Establish an Evening Wind-Down Routine

Give your nervous system a soft landing at night. Unplug. Dim the lights. Speak gratitude out loud. Reflect. Let your mind know the day is done, and so are you.

Journal Prompts: Build Your Peace Plan

1. What does being "grounded" feel like in my body?
2. What are three daily habits that help me feel safe, supported, and steady?
3. What part of my day needs more stillness, softness, or structure?

Affirmations: For the Woman Rooting Herself in Wholeness

- I begin each day by coming home to myself.
- My peace is not optional, it is essential.
- I have the power to slow down and stay present.
- The world can wait, my wellness cannot.
- Grounded women build empires with grace and clarity.

NOTES

CHAPTER 5

LOVE, RELATIONSHIPS & THE EMOTIONAL ROLLERCOASTER

Balancing entrepreneurship with a relationship, job, raising kids, grandkids, friendships, and every other relationship you must manage is something we barely talk about when it comes to being women who are building and running businesses. It's already hard as hell to make sure you have time for the people you love when you are out here hustling to make your dreams come true. We don't like to talk about the strained marriages, relationships, etc., that sometimes come along with the CEO life. Add bipolar disorder, anxiety and depression to the mix and you have potential for disaster.

That's exactly where I found myself. Struggling emotionally, angry, anxious, and lashing out at the people around me. Plus, I was just entering perimenopause, so I was a hot and moody mess, literally and figuratively.

Now, let's talk about the parts no one warns you about, you know, the stuff that no one mentions because it's just too uncomfortable or embarrassing. And people don't understand it anyway, right? Like trying to explain to someone you love that "I swear, I'm not mad at you, I love you, I'm just trying to survive my own brain today."

Or pulling back from a relationship, not because you don't care, (unless you really don't... that's a topic for another time though), but because you're afraid you'll fall apart and take them with you. Maybe you feel like they will judge you and leave you, so you hide your struggles and suffer in silence and alone.

Bipolar disorder, anxiety, and depression don't just affect your *mind*. No, they touch your heart and soul, and trickle into your romantic relationships, friendships, family dynamic, all of it, *especially* when you're a woman who leads, gives, and holds so much for others.

For a long time, I thought love meant hiding the hard parts of me. I tried to protect myself from the pain of accepting that this is part of my life, and I wanted to protect other people from the truth of my anxiety, depression, and mood swings.

But hiding only made the loneliness deeper. I had to come out of hiding, so I made the decision to actively pursue peace and total healing.

Here's what I learned: **if you must shrink, lie, or disappear to be loved, it's not love.**

Let's Talk About: Loving While Living with Mental Health Challenges

It's about choosing connection over fear. Learning how to communicate without shame. And pursuing love that *sees* you, not just the put together version of you. But, at the same time, you must be willing to share those vulnerable parts of you.

When I think of all the time I have spent convincing myself that no one cared or would understand me, I recognized I had created that narrative to protect myself from being judged. I never really gave people the chance to get to know that side because I would shut down and withdraw from the hard conversations. I would become angry and lash out instead of expressing how I was truly feeling when I was battling through mania or a depressive period.

You see, that's the thing about the mind of someone living with mental health disorders. We are wired differently and sometimes it takes a while for us to recognize when we are our own worst enemy. But the beauty of self-awareness and being intentional about your healing once you master your moods, you will notice the signs and can prepare for them before they take a toll on your relationships. You don't have to be afraid or ashamed sista, because the people that love you will love you no matter what. And the ones that don't, to hell with them, they are not for you anyway!

Three Tips for Navigating Relationships with Mental Health in the Mix:

Share From a Place of Self-Awareness, Not Shame

It's true you don't owe everyone an explanation about your mental health challenges and the behaviors that come with it, but the people who love you *deserve* your honesty. It can be hard to feel comfortable enough to be vulnerable to people and tell them what is really happening in your world. It's even harder when you're a black woman living in a world that expects you to take what the world throws at you in stride. Believe me, I get it, but I promise you that the people who truly love and respect you will understand and keep on loving you. Share your truth in small, clear ways. Start with "This is what I experience when I have manic or depressive episodes, and here's what helps me when it gets hard."

Set Boundaries with Love and Confidence

It is so important to set clear and unbreakable boundaries. Why? Because your mental health is not up for negotiation. Create space to regroup, disappear for a few hours, or the day when you need to. Protect your peace without apology. And avoid further explanation after you say no.

There is nothing to explain and nothing more to say after that.

Yes, it will be hard at first, especially when people are used to you giving in and not having boundaries. Let people know, listen, "I care about you deeply, and I also need time to reset." It's just that simple and you deserve that respect. If they can't honor your boundaries, show them the door.

Don't Date Potential, Date Capacity

Entrepreneurship is hard enough without the added stress of trying to date or maintain a relationship while doing it. If you are still on the dating scene, find someone who doesn't panic and flip out when your nervous system needs a minute. What you want is someone who supports, not rescues you. Someone who can walk with you *without* becoming your crutch.

Girl, you are not here to convince anyone how to love you and there's a big difference between *seeing the best in someone* and *hoping they'll grow into the person you need them to be.* Dating folks with potential just means falling in love with who someone *could* become, while ignoring who they *are.* When you live with bipolar disorder or other mental health challenges or are navigating a healing journey, you don't have the luxury (or the time) of waiting for someone to catch up emotionally, mentally, or spiritually.

Date capacity. That means choosing a partner who already has the emotional maturity, self-awareness, and stability to hold space for your full self, especially on your hard days. Capacity shows up in the little things: someone who doesn't take your quiet moments personally. Someone who listens without trying to fix. Someone who can sit with your sadness without feeling like they're drowning in it too.

You're not here to teach someone how to love you, you're here to be met, supported, and respected by someone who *already* knows how to offer healthy, consistent love. Choose the person who sees your power, understands your process, and doesn't flinch when your nervous system needs a minute to breathe. That's not a fixer. That's a partner.

Journal Prompts: Let Love Meet You Where You Are

1. Where do I still feel like I have to "perform wellness" in relationships?
2. What kind of love does my soul actually need?
3. How can I communicate my emotional needs without guilt or fear?

Affirmations: For the Woman Loving and Being Loved with Mental Health Challenges

- I am worthy of love, even in my darkest moments.

- My vulnerability is a bridge, not a burden.
- I choose relationships that honor my healing, not disrupt it.
- I can be loved *and* have boundaries.
- The right people don't run, they reach.

NOTES

PART 2

THE OUTER GAME...WORKING & WINNING AS A CEO WITH A MENTAL HEALTH CONDITION

CHAPTER 6

BUILDING A BUSINESS THAT HONORS YOUR BRAIN

For years, I built my business on burnout. No breaks. No boundaries. Just back-to-back launches, inbox anxiety, and breakdowns behind the scenes. There would be times when I could get things done and times when I would sit and stare blankly at my screen because my brain was in a fog.

I remember back when I was running my custom sweets business and would be so excited when I would get orders. Then, self-doubt would kick in and I would start telling myself that I wasn't a good enough baker, or that I wouldn't be able to decorate the cakes right.

Then came the panic, the heavy breathing, the heart beating out of my chest. I essentially would think myself right into anxiety. Then I wouldn't rest until I perfected the recipe, the decorating, and I mean right down to the box I was putting it in. I would get overwhelmed, but I kept going because that's what a good business owner does, right?

Yes, I thought success meant *pushing through* no matter how I felt. But here's what that got me: sleepless nights, panic attacks, and months of silence because I was too emotionally depleted to create anything.

But I finally said, "Girl, enough is enough!" Everything, and I do mean everything changed when I gave myself permission to build a business that works for who I really am, a brilliant, passionate, purpose-driven woman... who also happens to live with bipolar disorder, anxiety, and depression. And that's okay.

This chapter isn't about doing less. It's about doing what works for *you.*

Creating a Business Model That Supports Mental Wellness

No matter what you've heard from all the gurus, success is not just about what you build, it's about how you feel while building it. You are the CEO, and you get to design your systems, schedule, and services around *your capacity*, not by comparing yourself to other people and what success looks like for them.

Build a Brand That Serves Both Your Bank Account & Your Brain

There was a time when I would enter a manic period and didn't know or understand how to navigate and manage that energy. Hell, until a few years ago I had no idea what I was experiencing so I didn't recognize the triggers and symptoms.

Before my diagnosis in 2019, a manic episode for me would be extreme and reckless spending, risky sexual behavior, (way back in the day in my younger years), partying, drinking, and a few other things. There were times when I would spend hundreds, sometimes thousands of dollars, on shopping, or joining some program, and would regret it later after I came down from the high energy and realized what I had done.

After my diagnosis, I learned to notice when I am heading down the manic path and I now take that energy and put into improving my health by working out or growing my business by creating some awesome thing for a client. How? Because the mania that comes with bipolar disorder is a time when you are full of energy, ideas, creativity, and you feel like you can take over the world! I can create a marketing plan, presentation, write a book, and a million other things when I am in a manic period.

Instead of engaging in behavior that will eventually send me spiraling into depression if I'm not careful, I use my energy to grow my brand and make more money in my business.

Here's a few things you can do to turn those never-ending thoughts and ideas into something great!

Use Your High-Energy Windows Wisely

When your mood is stable, your thoughts are clear, and your motivation is high, *go all in.* These moments are gold for creators, entrepreneurs, and visionaries living with mental health conditions like anxiety, depression, or bipolar disorder. Don't waste your momentum scrolling or second-guessing. Use those green-light windows to batch content, record video, outline your next launch, or write your next email sequence. Think of it as building your own emergency fund, not for money, but for *momentum.* When your energy dips or life hits hard, you'll have work on deck that still reflects your brilliance, even when you're not at your best.

Systemize the Stress Points

Stress isn't just uncomfortable, it's costly. It's a sneaky thief that robs you of your clarity, confidence, and sometimes your capacity to keep going. I want you to take the time to narrow down and pinpoint your biggest stressors in your business. Which everyday tasks trigger your anxiety or drain your energy the fastest?

Is it the seemingly endless emails? Keeping up with social media trends and posting content? Client follow-ups? Collecting leads? No matter what it is, automate it, delegate it, or simplify it. We cannot let our business run us into the ground emotionally when there are tools out there to keep that from happening!

Yes, girl! Systems are self-care for CEOs. Tools like CRMs (Client Relationship Management software), like Monday or Salesforce, content schedulers like Later or Planoly, and email autoresponders like Mailchimp or Constant Contact, can help you show up professionally and consistently *without* needing to be "on" all the time. You didn't build your brand just to feel overwhelmed by it. Let your systems hold you down when your nervous system needs rest.

Design for Flexibility, Not Just Hustle

Okay Sis, it's time to stop building like you're a machine. You're not, and your business shouldn't treat you like one. If your model only works when you're constantly producing, posting, or showing up live, it's time to rethink it. It is imperative for your well-being that you scrap that and rebuild with *flexibility* in mind. Spread out your calendar. Make room for rest and mental resets. Create offers that can run without your presence every hour of every day, like downloadable courses, eBooks, digital templates, or evergreen funnels. Flexibility isn't a luxury, it's a *lifeline.* Hustle culture will burn you out, but a flexible business will give you space to *breathe* and still get paid!

Journal Prompts: Reimagine How You Work

1. What parts of my business feel emotionally heavy or overstimulating?
2. What would a business built around *my* energy patterns look like?
3. Where can I give myself more grace, space, or support right now?

Affirmations: For the CEO Creating from Self-Awareness, Not Burnout

- I lead a business that honors my mental, emotional, and energetic needs.
- Rest is not a reward, it's a requirement.
- I design success on my own terms, not hustle culture's expectations.
- I can serve powerfully without sacrificing my peace.
- My business works *because* I protect my wellness, not despite it.

NOTES

CHAPTER 7

MENTAL HEALTH IN LEADERSHIP

There used to be a time when I could turn it "on" like a switch. Camera on. Smile up. Voice steady. Business mode activated. But behind that screen? My mind was racing, and I was unraveling.

The world claps for and celebrates the woman who is strong but rarely makes space for the woman who *needs* strength. And when you're a woman in leadership with bipolar disorder, anxiety, or depression, the pressure to show up perfectly is *crushing.*

For years, I believed I had to compartmentalize, you know, business over here, mental health over there. But here's the truth: I am not two people. I am one whole woman. And now

I lead better, love deeper, and create more powerfully because I stopped pretending and started honoring my humanity and womanhood.

Being Seen Without Hiding Your Struggles

Leadership isn't about always being "on," no, it's about being *real* and being *present*, with yourself and with others. You don't need to have it all together to be impactful. You don't have to pretend the hard parts of your story don't exist. True leadership invites authenticity, not performance.

You get to be transparent without being exposed. You can show up and share your truth while still honoring your privacy. Boundaries and vulnerability *can* co-exist. And when they do, your influence becomes even more powerful, because people don't connect to your perfection, they connect to your *presence.*

Here are three ways to protect your mental health as a leader without hiding what makes you human:

Protecting Your Mental Health as a Leader

Lead With Honesty, Not a Highlight Reel

We live in a crazy time of Tik Tok videos, Facebook stories, and Instagram reels, and the world wants to see everything! It can become overwhelming and may leave you feeling like to have to tell all your business to get the attention of your audience and make the sale. I'm here to tell you that you're not obligated to share every detail of your struggle, but you *can* choose to lead from a place of honesty. That might sound like, "Today is a slower day for me," or "This week I'm prioritizing mental rest. Being a leader doesn't mean curating a flawless image, it means showing up as your full authentic, wonderful self.

Share what you've learned, not just what you've achieved. People crave real connection, and when you show what healthy vulnerability looks like, you give others permission to do the same. Your courage to be human creates safer spaces for others to grow, too.

Speak Your Needs Before Crisis Hits

Listen sis, your power lies in preparation, not perfection. Don't wait until you're overwhelmed, burned out, and on the verge of a breakdown to ask for a break or support. Let the people around you, whether it's your team, clients, audience, or collaborators, know what helps you function at your best. And don't be afraid or ashamed to do so. If you are surrounded by the right folks, they will understand and support you because they want to see you succeed.

Clear expectations prevent confusion and protect your peace. For example: "I typically respond within 48 hours," or "If I'm in a low-energy cycle, I'll delegate or reschedule." This kind of proactive communication isn't a weakness, it's wisdom. It builds trust and creates sustainable leadership.

Redefine What "Professional" Looks Like

You are the blueprint. The old played out rules don't apply anymore. Professionalism isn't about being polished at the expense of your well-being, it's about showing up with purpose, not performance.

Whether you're in sweats on your Zoom call with a candle burning, or leading a team call from your couch, your presence and preparation matter more than your presentation. You are redefining leadership by showing that mental wellness IS part of the business model, not something you have to hide.

Journal Prompts: Reflect on Your Leadership Identity

1. Where am I still hiding parts of myself to seem "strong?"
2. What would it feel like to lead without a mask?
3. How can I model mental wellness for others in my business or community?

Affirmations: For the Woman Who Leads with Bold Vulnerability

- I am a powerful leader, even when I feel tender, tired, or unsure.
- My transparency is an act of courage, not weakness.
- I do not have to hide to be respected.

- I set the tone by honoring myself first.
- I lead from my truth, and that is enough.

NOTES

CHAPTER 8

The Myth of Balance & the Truth About Capacity

I know you've heard this a thousand times: *"You just need more balance."* Am I right?

But what does that even mean? What are we doing here? Balance between what and what? Business and family? Hustle and healing. Passion and peace?

No! Social media and the internet in general have some of us thinking we must keep up with everything and everyone if we want to be successful. That's a false narrative that will keep you stressed out and overwhelmed if you're not careful.

Let go of the pressure to keep up with someone else's pace. This is your journey, your rhythm, your time, and your mental health requires a different kind of leadership, one rooted in *self-awareness,* not self-comparison. Being consistent does not mean you have to do the same thing every day; it simply means showing up in alignment with what you have to give.

You don't need more balance; you need to trust your *bandwidth.* To honor your energy, your emotions, and your nervous system without guilt. Because when you work *with* your capacity, not against it, and not try to go around it, you make room for your best work to come through, even in seasons of struggle.

What I've learned, (the hard way), is that **balance is a moving target**, and you will not lock it down! Especially when you add your unpredictable energy, moods, emotions, and needs.

And guess what? That's not failure. In fact, that's the art of womanhood. That's being human.

You weren't meant to do *all the things all the time.* No ma'am! You were created to move in *seasons.* And the key to thriving isn't balancing everything, it's knowing what you can handle and honoring your **capacity**.

Here are 3 truths about capacity that shifted everything for me—and they just might do the same for you:

Capacity Changes Daily…And That's Okay

Your energy, focus, and creativity will fluctuate, especially if you're navigating bipolar, anxiety, depression, or any condition that affects your emotional or physical baseline. Make peace with it. Why? Because some days, you'll feel like the badass powerhouse you are, while other days, it might take everything you have just to respond to a text or show up on a Zoom call.

That fluctuation doesn't make you unreliable, once again, it means you are human!

So, try this, start your day with a check-in:

What does my mind, body, and heart need today?

What do I have the capacity to give today?

That one moment of awareness can keep you from slipping into burnout disguised as ambition.

You Can't Pour from an Empty Cup, or a Cracked One

No matter how big your dreams are, they can't come at the cost of your health. Build in buffer time. Cancel things without guilt. Say no more often. It's not just about rest. It's about repair.

You may be running on fumes, and still trying to push through because of deadlines, clients, or internal pressure to perform.

But if your "cup" is cracked, and you're leaking energy, peace, or joy, you won't be able to sustain yourself long-term.

So, build in buffer time. Cancel without guilt. Say no with confidence. Your calendar should have just as much *white space* as it does checkboxes and colors. None of those deadlines, meetings, or appointments will matter if you are too worn down to function.

This isn't about lowering your standards; it's about *protecting your sustainability.* You don't have to earn your rest. You need it to rise.

Redefine Productivity as *Alignment*

Having a productive day isn't just crossing things off your to-do list. It's creating results that matter, in ways that don't drain your soul, and have you wondering why you even started your business in the first place. Some days, productivity is launching. Other days, it's taking the day off to chill at a park or take a walk by the water, or simply saying, "Today, I'm prioritizing my peace." Each is valid, powerful, and progress.

The world may reward hustle, but your *healing* requires harmony. Stop chasing the illusion of constantly doing more, shift your focus to doing what matters.

Journal Prompts: Reconnect With Your True Capacity

1. When was the last time I honored what my mind and body needed?

2. What areas of my life am I overcommitting to right now?
3. What would shift if I worked from my capacity instead of guilt?

Affirmations: For the Woman Who's Done Overcommitting & Undervaluing Herself

- My value isn't tied to how much I produce.
- I honor my capacity with grace, not guilt.
- Saying "no" is how I say "yes" to my peace.
- I choose alignment over exhaustion.
- I lead from a place of wisdom, not pressure.

NOTES

CHAPTER 9

Boundaries, Burnout, and Brave Breaks

I Used to Wear Burnout Like a Badge

Listen, there was a time when I believed being exhausted all the time was a sign I was doing something right. Especially when I was new to the world of digital entrepreneurship. The endless late nights, back-to-back Zoom calls, and saying "yes" when I knew damn well my body and mind were begging me to say "no." I thought pushing through made me strong, that resilience meant constantly proving I could handle more.

I was suffering from a terrible case of imposter syndrome, (that I completely created in my own mind, by the way), and I felt like I had to say yes to everyone and everything to prove how authentic I was. But all it really made me was *empty, tired, and broke.*

There wasn't just some single dramatic moment where it all fell apart. No, it was gradual...feeling drained before the day even started, showing up with a fake smile and a heavy heart, losing passion for the work I used to love. One day, I sat in silence and realized: "Girl, are you nuts?" You don't just deserve rest. *You better require it.*

Boundaries aren't walls to shut people out. They're *bridges back to yourself.*

Especially as a woman CEO living, working, and thriving with bipolar disorder, anxiety, or depression, boundaries are not optional. They are your safety net. They keep you from falling all the way off when life, business, or your emotions get too heavy.

Making Rest and Boundaries Are Non-Negotiable

Burnout isn't a sign you're weak or undisciplined. It's a sign you've been giving too much of yourself to things that drain you, instead of things that are fulfilling. You don't have to do less, just do less of what doesn't serve your soul.

Here are three ways to set boundaries and avoid burnout while building a business that honors both your bank account *and* your well-being:

Setting Boundaries & Avoiding Burnout

Identify What Sucks You Dry

Before you can protect your energy, you must check yourself to know where it's leaking. Think about this for a second, then answer this question. Who or what leaves me feeling exhausted, anxious, or resentful?

Clean up your calendar. Look at your client list, your projects, your habits. Notice the patterns. Is it certain conversations? Too many notifications? Overbooking yourself?

Write it all down. Energy leaks lead to emotional bankruptcy. Emotional bankruptcy leads to financial mayhem. Plug the holes before you crash and take your business down with you.

Create a "Break Plan" Before You Need One

Waiting until you're overwhelmed to take a break is like waiting until your car breaks down to get an oil change.

Build intentional breaks into your schedule *now*, yes, RIGHT NOW, before your body or mind forces you to.

That could mean:

- 10 minutes of silence between meetings
- One mental health day every week (self-care Saturday)

- A quarterly weekend where you fully unplug (book a room if you can)

Put it on your calendar. Treat it like any other non-negotiable business meeting and stick to it.

Communicate Your Boundaries Like a CEO

Your boundaries only work if people *know* them. Please stop expecting people to read your mind or know what you want unless you have told them.

Be clear, speak confidently, and stand on business:

"I don't take calls after 6 PM."

"I need 48 hours to respond to emails."

"I'm unavailable on weekends."

You're not being difficult. You don't have to be sorry or apologize for it. You're leading by example. Running a business and being professional doesn't mean folks get 24/7 access. People respect what you reinforce, and when you honor your own limits, it teaches others to do the same. You know what they say...you teach people how to treat you.

Journal Prompts: Protect Your Peace, Reclaim Your Time

1. Where in my life or business am I allowing energy leaks right now?

2. What boundary do I need to set today to protect my mental wellness?
3. How do I feel when I honor my need for rest without guilt?

Affirmations: For the Woman Who Knows Her Worth and Protects Her Energy

- My peace is priceless. I protect it boldly.
- Boundaries are a form of self-love and leadership.
- Rest is a business strategy, not a weakness.
- I release the need to prove myself through overworking.
- I honor my yes and my no with equal confidence.

NOTES

CHAPTER 10

THE TEAM THAT KEEPS ME TOGETHER

There used to be a time in my life when my favorite phrase, my automatic response to everything, was:

"I got it."

Need something done? I got it.

Feeling overwhelmed? It's okay. I got it.

On the edge of burnout, spiraling emotionally? Yup... I got it.

That backwards mindset didn't make me stronger. It was quite the opposite; it almost broke me.

Here's what nobody tells women like us:

You can be powerful, brilliant, resourceful and *still* need help, especially when you're building or running a business while juggling your bipolar disorder, anxiety, or depression symptoms. Stop trying to carry both the weight of leadership *and* healing on your own shoulders, sis.

There is no prize for carrying everything alone. There is only exhaustion, isolation, and eventually, collapse and burnout. That's it.

I had to learn the hard way, out of necessity, because it certainly was not a luxury, how to build my CEO Mental Health Squad: The personal and professional team that holds me down, lifts me up, and reminds me that I'm never in this thing by myself. I could not have made it this far without these powerful, supportive women in my circle.

Whether you're running a business, raising a family, or both, (which is usually the case) you deserve the same.

Building Your Circle of Support

Every woman CEO needs a system of support that nurtures both her *strategy* and her *soul.* From therapists to coaches, assistants, accountability partners to prayer partners, this isn't about weakness. You need a solid team of sistas to keep you on your toes, and step in when you can't stand on those toes.

It's about wisdom. The wisdom to know that you will not make it to the next level of your journey on your own. You weren't built to do it all. And you don't have to.

Members of Your CEO Mental Health Squad

Your Emotional Support Team

This is the team that holds your heart. It could be a therapist, your life coach, a good girlfriend, or a support group, these are the people you can show up to with no filter. No business talk. No pretending. No having to be "on".

I was so blessed to have been sent a network of women who hold me accountable, but who will pray, talk, or just listen to me when I need them. No questions asked. It was hard for me at first because I was not used to this type of support, until I came around and accepted all the love and support they had for me. You deserve the same.

You need spaces and people where and to whom you don't have to explain or justify your feelings. You should be able to say, "I'm not okay today," and be met with care, not judgment.

What's the point of building your empire and legacy if you lose yourself along the way?

Your Business Support Team

This is the crew that keeps things moving when you don't have the energy or capacity to.

Think of virtual assistants, project managers, accountants, social media managers, marketing managers, and anyone who helps take tasks off your plate so you can avoid overwhelm and focus on what matters most.

Remember this, delegation is not just about scaling. It's about self-preservation.

Your mental health and your business should not be in competition with each other. Your business should *support* your mental health and that means getting help when you need it.

Your Spiritual or Grounding Support Team

For me, that's my faith circle: prayer partners, women I can call on for spiritual guidance and encouragement. Sometimes it's quiet mornings with meditation, journaling, and scripture. Other times it's a long drive out to the country or being down by the river.

For you, it might look a little different: yoga, breathwork, therapy, nature walks. Whatever helps you stay grounded and connected to your Source.

Your emotional wellness and spiritual wellness should go hand in hand and work together to keep you together. Why? Because one holds the mind. The other holds the soul.

Journal Prompts: Build Your Team with Intention

- Who do I currently rely on for emotional and mental support?
- What business tasks could I delegate to protect my energy and focus?
- Where am I still trying to carry things alone—and what's stopping me from asking for help?

Take time to sit with these questions. Your next level doesn't just require more effort sista, it requires more *support.*

Affirmations: For the Woman Who Knows She's Strong—But Not Meant to Do It Alone

- I am supported, even when I don't see it.
- Asking for help is a power move, not a weakness.
- I deserve a team that honors my vision and my wellness.
- My success is a collective effort—I'm not in this by myself.
- I release the belief that I must carry it all on my own.

NOTES

PART 3

THE BECOMING... BEING UNAPOLOGETICALLY HER

CHAPTER 11

Making Peace with Your Messy Middle

We love a good before-and-after story, don't we? It's always amazing to see how another woman worked to change her life and live her dreams! Before: struggling. After: thriving, healed, successful. When you see those side-by-side pictures it almost looks like it happened overnight doesn't it?

Those edited and polished reels make it easy to believe that life is one big transformation story with a beautiful, perfect ending. But what we don't see is the part in between, that's where the real transformation is happening. Right there in the middle.

The middle is messy girl. It's uncertain. It's uneven. It's funky as hell. And for me, that's where most of my transformation has unfolded. Those sleepless prayer filled nights and emotional early mornings when I was up writing, talking to God, and meditating on His word and promise. That's where my transformation was unfolding, and of course it happened before anyone saw the results.

The middle is waking up some days feeling powerful, focused, and ready to lead and change the world and waking up other days wondering how I'll even make it out of bed.

It's building a business while managing bipolar disorder, anxiety, or depression symptoms that threatened to take me out if I wasn't vigilant about my healing. The messy middle is getting it wrong or at least feeling like you did and wondering if you will ever get it right.

It's growing, backsliding, learning, trying again.

It took me years to understand that healing isn't linear. Success isn't linear. Hell no! It's messy, funky, and can sometimes be gut wrenching in the middle.

There are still days I feel unstoppable... and days I feel stuck, overwhelmed, or invisible.

But you know what, both are real. Both are valid. Both are part of my story.

If you're reading this while standing in your own middle, girl, *don't rush through it.*

Don't disqualify yourself because things aren't perfect yet.

There's gold here.

There's growth here. There's grit.

And there's grace.

Owning Your Journey as It Is…The Good, Bad, and The Ugly

I finally figured out that your life does not have to be all good before it's worth sharing. In fact, that's what people want to see and hear about. The tough part.

Your leadership doesn't have to be flawless before it's real.

You can live, love, and lead while still becoming.

You can create impact even while you're figuring things out.

The messy middle isn't a detour baby. It *is* the road. Your road.

Making Peace with Your Process

Girl, Stop Measuring Yourself by the Finish Line.

We've been conditioned to ask: "How far do I still have to go?" "Are we almost there?" But that question has a way of creating self-doubt and steals your joy. It makes you focus on what you haven't done yet and ignores how far you've already come and what you have accomplished so far.

For the longest time, especially when I first stepped into this world of online and digital entrepreneurship, I would be so focused on "getting to the next level" that I completely ignored and forgot about how far I had come.

I would be looking at where I thought everyone else was, and felt lost and inadequate, like I would never "catch up." That was so detrimental to my growth and healing, because I had no business worrying about what anyone else was doing. I had to learn to keep my eyes on my own prize.

Don't get caught up in that mess, try this instead:

"How far have I come from where I started?" "What was I doing this time last year?" Take a look back at your old journal entries and see how your mindset has changed.

Your progress isn't always loud or dramatic. Sometimes, progress is simply showing up for yourself again. Choosing not to give up.

The bottom line is that if all you did today was get out of bed, or answer one email, text one person back, or pause for five deep breaths, that's forward motion.

Celebrate Your Quiet Victories

Look sis, not every win will show up as a big check.

Sometimes, the win is posting content when you don't feel like it.

Sometimes, it's taking a mental health break before you crash instead of waiting until after the crash happens.

Sometimes, it's choosing to journal instead of snapping! It's okay to give yourself credit where it's due. Why? Because every small step matters. Those quiet victories add up to something powerful over time.

Let Go of Perfection and Embrace Practice

Healing is a practice.

Leadership is a practice.

Growth is a practice.

You don't "arrive" at perfect. You get *better*...one moment, one choice, one day at a time.

It's okay to show up unfinished.

It's okay to launch that program or share your story before you feel fully "ready."

Your middle is just as meaningful as your before and after.

Journal Prompts: Honor Your Middle

- What progress have I made that I haven't given myself credit for?
- Where am I still waiting for things to be "perfect" before I show up fully?

- How can I give myself more grace in this season?
- Set aside quiet time with these prompts. Let them remind you that growth is happening—*even now.*

Affirmations: For the Woman Becoming in Real Time

- I honor my journey, even in its unfinished chapters.
- Progress is enough. I am enough.
- I release the need for perfection. I choose presence instead.
- Every step I take forward matters, no matter how small.
- My middle is meaningful. My story is still unfolding.

NOTES

CHAPTER 12

Your Story Is Someone's Survival Guide

For a long time, I carried my struggles in silence because I thought no one cared. I mean, who would want to hear about little old me anyway? So, I kept it all to myself, all of it. The anxiety. Depressive spirals. The sad days when I felt completely unworthy, feeling like I didn't belong in the rooms I had worked so hard to enter.

Yup, I convinced myself no one needed to know; that showing my cracks would make me look weak, and sharing my truth would somehow overshadow my credibility as a leader, as a CEO, as a woman other women looked up to.

So, I kept on telling myself:

"Once I get it all together, once I clean up my messy middle... then I'll share."

"Once I'm healed and whole... once I'm successful enough... once I make more money... once I don't feel this way anymore."

But here's what I've learned, what life forced me to understand:

There is no such thing as having your shit "all together."

There is no perfect earth-shattering moment when your story becomes put together enough, clean enough, polished enough to share.

The story you're sitting on right now, you know the one I mean, the one that feels too messy, too painful, too crazy is *exactly* the story another sista needs to hear. She's waiting for you to share it; she just doesn't know it yet.

The bottom line is that it's not about being perfect. It's about being real. That's what sets people free.

Every single time I've opened up publicly about my mental health as a CEO, as a woman living with bipolar disorder, anxiety, and depression, I get messages from women saying: "Thank you, I thought it was just me."

A few months ago, I was at the launch of my last book, "The Second Wind," and I shared some things about my struggles with my mental health. So many of the women there came up to me afterwards and thanked me for being so transparent. I can't tell you how good it felt to speak to these women who thought they were all alone in their mental health journey.

But, I promise, it's *never* just you. And your story might be a crack of light in someone else's darkness.

That's why I wrote *Don't Call Me Crazy, Call Me CEO*.

Because we don't have to hide anymore. We don't have to shrink anymore. We don't have to settle anymore.

We can lead, heal, and rise, all at the same time.

Owning Your Story to Empower Others

Contrary to what the digital world may have you think, you don't have to be famous to make an impact. Nope. You just must be honest, and unapologetically you. Here's how to do it with clarity, intention, and authenticity:

Three Ways to Share Your Story Authentically

Share From the Healed Scar, Not the Open Wound

It's true that when we're in the middle of a breakdown, our emotions are raw, unfiltered, and sometimes uncontrolled. That's not always the best time to put our story out to the world. Why? Because it's pretty hard to see the lessons while you're still living them.

When you share from the scar you are giving yourself space to heal, reflect, and gain perspective before you open up to others. No, it doesn't mean waiting until you're 100% "healed," it only means sharing from a place where your words can offer clarity instead of confusion or hurt.

Consider this:

Instead of posting, "I'm spiraling right now, and I don't know what to do." You might share, "Last month I hit a rough patch with my mental health. Here's what I learned and what helped me through it..."

This way, you're offering wisdom, not just unloading emotion.

Focus on Service, Not Sympathy

When you tell your story, make it about who it can help, not about seeking validation or garnering sympathy. Your vulnerability is valuable, but it becomes *transformative* when you pair it with purpose.

Ask yourself before you share:

- "Will this story help another woman feel less alone?"
- "What lesson can I pass on?"

Highlighting service keeps your message clear and empowering and protects you and your audience from getting stuck in never-ending cycles of pain without growth. When you post about surviving burnout or battling depression, don't just stop at what happened, share how you made it through, the tools you used, and where you are now.

Be Specific and Relatable

The real power in storytelling isn't in the general "I struggled narrative." It's in the details that make people nod their heads and say, "Wow, that's me."

People connect with specifics:

- The 3 a.m. panic attack.
- The client calls you dragged yourself through while mentally checked out.
- The moment you finally asked for help after holding it all in for months.

The more honest and specific you are, the more universal your message becomes—because it touches on things people *feel* but don't always say.

Instead of: "It was a hard season."

Say: "There were days I couldn't open my laptop without my chest tightening. So, I set my calendar to 'do not disturb' for a week, and I learned my business didn't fall apart just because I took a breath."

Journal Prompts

1. What part of my story do I usually keep hidden?
2. How has hearing someone else's truth helped me in the past?
3. What message do I want people to take away from my journey?

Affirmations

- My story has power, even in its unfinished parts.
- I speak my truth with boldness and purpose.
- Someone is waiting for my testimony to start their healing.
- I don't need perfection to inspire—I only need honesty.
- My voice matters. My story matters. I matter.

NOTES

CHAPTER 13

THE FIERCE, FEMININE, FEARLESS WAY FORWARD

For so long, I was in survival mode. I was never really living or thriving, I was just existing, surviving.

Keeping my business hanging on by a thread. Keeping my emotions in check. Keeping up appearances. Keeping up with everyone else.

But I reached a point where I realized: *Girl, you are forty-seven years old, this isn't about surviving anymore.*

It's about *thriving*, as a CEO, as a boss, as a woman, as a whole human being.

Living with bipolar disorder, anxiety, and depression hasn't stopped me from building businesses, writing books, leading women, or creating a life I love. But it has required me to do it a lot differently than what many of these leadership books teach.

I had to let go of the hustle-for-approval mindset that had me stressed out and feeling inadequate.

I had to stop believing that perfection equaled power. And that stress equaled success.

Instead, I learned to lead from:

- Grace, not grind.
- Power, not perfection.
- Alignment, not outside approval.

The fierce, feminine, fearless way to leadership isn't about plowing your way through every obstacle. It's about knowing your rhythm and cadence.

It's about knowing when to push, when to pull, when to pause, and when to protect your peace at all costs.

It's about creating success that feels *good* to you and is good for you, not success that only looks good on the outside while draining your soul.

Now, you get to decide:

What does success mean *to me*?

What do I really want my life to look and feel like?

Who cares what social media says. We are no longer measuring success that way. No. Not based on family expectations, but based on what makes your soul sing, feel alive and whole.

It's Based on Living Boldly and Leading Authentically Long Term

Girl, this isn't just a season. It's your season.

This isn't just a "healing phase," it's your healing!

This is a *lifestyle. Not a temporary fix.*

You are not building a business so you can crash out and recover.

You're building a life you don't want or need a vacation from.

A life that makes room for your brilliance *and* your bad days.

A life where your power and your softness get to exist.

A life where you lead boldly. Live fully. And never feel like you must choose between your mental health and your mission.

Core Practices to Carry Forward

These aren't just your typical leadership hacks or self-care tips. No ma'am! These are the same anchors and practices I used to get through my mental health struggles, anchors that keep you steady, especially when business, life, or your own emotions feel unpredictable. Whether you're scaling a business or just trying to hold yourself together through a tough season, these practices help you lead from a place of wholeness, not depletion.

Ground Yourself Daily

Prayer. Meditation. Journaling. Silence.

It doesn't need to look like anyone else's routine, but it does need to be *yours*.

When you're leading, creating, and serving others, it's easy to lose connection with yourself. That's why grounding isn't optional, it's a vital necessity.

Whether it's five minutes or fifty, create a daily ritual that brings you back to center, *Back to Her.*

Ask yourself these questions:

- What do I need right now?
- How am I feeling today?
- Where do I need to release control?

As a woman CEO managing mental health challenges, your nervous system needs consistency. This is non-negotiable. Your mind needs stillness every day. Your spirit needs anchoring every day. Make room on your daily calendar for your grounding routine, no matter how busy or messy the day gets.

Check In with Capacity Regularly

Your energy, focus, and creativity will shift, and that's not failure. It's life. And that's okay.

Yes, there will be days when you feel clear, confident, and ready to run the world. And there will be days when the simplest things feel overwhelming. That doesn't mean you've lost your momentum. It only means you need to adjust.

Check in with yourself consistently:

- What's my real capacity today?
- What can I move, delegate, or pause?
- Is my calendar serving me, or stressing me out?

Build flexibility into everything: your schedule, your offers, your team communication. Protecting your peace isn't a side note or occasional luxury, it's part of your business strategy.

A business that only works when you're at 100% isn't sustainable. Make sure your systems, team, and mindset leave room for your CEO self-care days.

Lead From Who You Are, Not Who You Think You Should Be

You don't have to lead like anyone else. You have your own purpose and mission; all you need to do is honor that. You don't have to be the loudest voice in the room to make your presence known and felt.

You don't need to lead like the perfect leader with the perfect brand. You don't even have to lead like the version of yourself you outgrew years ago.

Your power isn't in copying someone else's rhythm or voice.

Your power is in your *own* voice. Your own truth. Your own story.

So, it's time to give yourself permission to let go of outdated cookie cutter expectations, whether they come from your industry, your family, or even your past self.

Leadership, especially as a woman, isn't about fitting into a mold. It's about breaking them and creating new space for yourself and others.

The more authentic you are, the more magnetic you become, not just to clients or followers, but to the life and peace you've been working so hard to build.

Journal Prompts

1. What does my version of fierce, feminine, fearless leadership look like?
2. What old beliefs about success or leadership am I ready to release?
3. How will I continue to protect my mental wellness as I grow?

Affirmations

- I lead with grace, power, and authenticity.
- My mental health is part of my leadership, not separate from it.
- I give myself permission to thrive, not just survive.
- Every step I take forward is a declaration of my worth.
- I am fierce. I am feminine. I am fearless, and I am free.

NOTES

YOUR JOURNEY, YOUR POWER

If you've made it this far, it means you're ready, not just to survive, but to lead, love, and live with your whole self.

This guide wasn't about teaching you how to be someone else. It was about reminding you of who you already are:

A woman of strength. A woman of grace. A woman of vision.

With or without the diagnosis, *you are still unapologetically HER* Bipolar disorder, anxiety, and depression may walk with you, but they damn sure don't define you.

You define you, sis.

Keep building your business. Keep nurturing your relationships.

Keep choosing yourself, every single day.

You've got this. And you are never alone in it.

FINAL LETTER TO THE READER

Dear Sister CEO,

I wrote this book for the version of me who felt completely alone. Now, I'm sharing it with the woman sitting at her desk, smiling on the outside, falling apart on the inside. For the leader who doesn't always feel strong but keeps showing up anyway.

If that's you, I see you Sista. I respect you. And I want you to know:

You do not have to choose between your healing and your hustle.

You do not have to be perfect to be powerful.

And you don't have to carry it all by yourself.

Your story matters. Your voice matters.

Keep leading. Keep healing. Keep becoming.

I am rooting for you always.

With fierce love and respect,

Angela M. Mitchell

MENTAL HEALTH RESOURCE LIST

Emergency Resources

- National Suicide Prevention Lifeline (U.S.): 988 (call or text)
- Crisis Text Line: Text HOME to 741741
- SAMHSA National Helpline: 1-800-662-HELP (4357)

Therapy & Support Platforms

- BetterHelp (www.betterhelp.com)
- Therapy for Black Girls (www.therapyforblackgirls.com)
- Open Path Collective (www.openpathcollective.org)

Mental Health & Leadership Communities

- NAMI (National Alliance on Mental Illness): www.nami.org
- The Loveland Foundation (therapy support for Black women): www.thelovelandfoundation.org

THE CEO CRISIS TOOLKIT

When You Feel Overwhelmed, Do This First:

- Stop. Breathe. Ground yourself. 4-7-8 Breathing Method: Inhale 4 counts, hold 7 counts, exhale 8 counts.
- Step away from screens. Go outside or change your environment.
- Text or call someone on your mental health squad. Use your support system.

Essential Items to Keep Close:

- A journal and pen
- Affirmation cards or post it reminders
- Emergency contact list
- Water and a nourishing snack
- Your favorite grounding playlist

Non-Negotiable Reminders:

- This feeling is temporary. It will pass.
- You are allowed to pause. Your business will wait.
- You are not alone. Reach out. Speak up.

NOTES

NOTES

NOTES

ABOUT THE AUTHOR

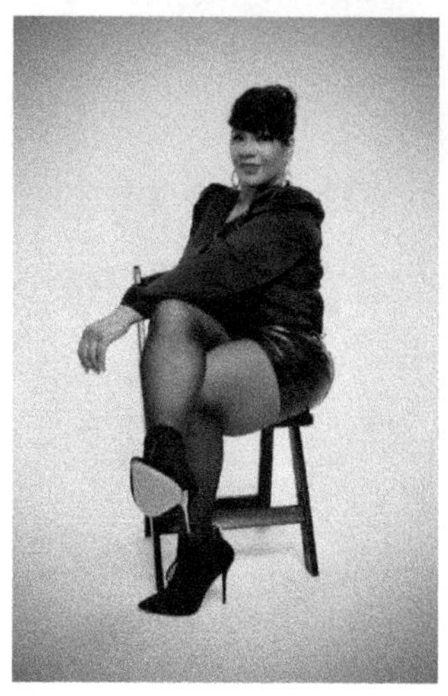

Angela M. Mitchell is an international bestselling author, certified master life and business coach, and digital marketing strategist. As the founder of *Back To Her*, Angela empowers high-achieving women entrepreneurs, coaches, and authors to reignite their passion, rediscover their purpose, and reinvent their lives and businesses from the inside out.

Diagnosed with bipolar disorder, anxiety, and depression in 2019, Angela turned her personal struggles into a movement—showing women worldwide that mental health challenges do not disqualify them from building successful businesses, living boldly, or leading with purpose.

Through books, workshops, coaching programs, and live events, Angela teaches practical strategies for business growth, brand visibility, and digital marketing while emphasizing mental wellness and authentic leadership.

When she's not coaching clients or hosting her *Courageous Conversations* blog and podcast, Angela can be found writing, creating digital products, or sharing her journey across social media platforms to inspire women to show up unmasked, unapologetic, and unstoppable.

To connect with Angela or learn more about her work, visit:

www.backtoher.com

Instagram: @angela_m_mitchell97

Facebook: Angela M Mitchell

TikTok: @angelammitchell

www.ingramcontent.com/pod-product-compliance
Lightning Source LLC
LaVergne TN
LVHW011029110826
845149LV00015B/3346